Big Book of
Knit Hats
& Scarves
for Everyone

Table of Contents

Introduction

Beginning knitters often learn to knit scarves because they're quick and easy to complete. But don't abandon scarves just because you're an accomplished knitter! This amazing collection of knit hats and scarves contains so many great projects, you'll want to knit them all. You can knit for yourself, babies and kids, men and women, friends and family—no matter their style or location.

You'll find projects that are easy to knit, with basic stitches and few color changes. You'll be inspired by the projects that are a little more complex, with new stitches and a variety of colors and types of yarns. And you'll be delighted with the variety, because there truly is something for everyone.

Jazz up your office wardrobe with Diamond Twist Scarf on page 20, Fringed Scarf on page 16, Angel Hair Scarf on page 18 and Striped Tiptop Hats on page 51.

Add glitz to that little black dress with Evening Intrigue Scarf on page 19, Shimmering Scarf on page 24 and Chic Cowl & Cuffs on page 30.

Chase the chill on those nippy winter days with Warm Ribbed Scarf on page 9, Holiday Warmer on page 10 and Cozy Amethyst Scarf on page 14.

So pick one of these fast and fun projects (it won't be hard!), grab your favorite knitting needles and some colorful yarn, and start knitting.

Stunning Scarves

Designs from Patons Yarns

Choose your favorite length and jazz up
your look with these scarves with pizzazz!

- Bulky weight nylon eyelash
  yarn (77 yds/50g per ball):
  1 ball pink fiesta
- Size 19 (15mm) needles or
  size needed to obtain gauge

Long Scarf

- Super bulky acrylic novelty
  yarn (85 yds/100g per ball):
  2 balls mango or peacock
- Bulky weight nylon eyelash
  yarn (77 yds/50g per ball):
  2 balls salsa or blue
- Size 19 (15mm) needles or
  size needed to obtain gauge

Gauge

6 sts and 12 rows = 4 inches/
10cm in garter st with
1 strand of each color
held tog
Gauge is not critical to
this project.

Scarf

With 1 strand of each yarn tog,
cast on 11 sts.

Work in garter st until scarf
measures 38 (77) inches, ending
with a RS row.

Bind off knitwise. ■

Skill Level ◼◻◻◻ BEGINNER

Finished Size

Short (long): Approx 7 x 38
(7 x 77) inches

Materials

Short Scarf
- Super bulky acrylic novelty
  yarn (85 yds/100g per ball):
  1 ball hot pink

6
SUPER BULKY

Greek Eyelash Scarf

Design by E.J. Slayton

Enhance your favorite outfit with a stylish scarf that is very quick to knit.

Skill Level ■□□□ BEGINNER

Finished Size
Approx 5 x 74 inches

Materials
- D.K. weight yarn (98 yds/50g per ball): 2 balls blue blend
- Size 9 (5.5mm) needles

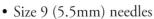

Gauge
Approx 8 sts = 4 inches/10cm in garter st
Gauge is not critical to this project.

Special Abbreviation
M1 (Make 1): Inc by k1 in top of st in row below.

Pattern Notes
With yarn in front, sl first st of every row purlwise, take yarn to back between needles for next st.

Use a safety pin or scrap of contrasting yarn to mark RS of fabric.

Designer suggests joining new skein of yarn by overlapping new and old strands by about 1½ inches, and stitching overlap with needle and matching sewing thread.

Scarf
Cast on 4 sts.

Row 1 (RS): Sl 1, M1, knit to end.
Row 2: Sl 1, knit to end.
Rep Rows 1 and 2 until there are 21 sts, then rep Row 2 until scarf measures approx 67 inches from beg or 7 inches less than desired length.

Shape end
Row 1 (RS): Sl 1, knit to last 3 sts, k2tog, k1.
Row 2: Sl 1, knit to end.
Rep Rows 1 and 2 until 4 sts rem, ending with Row 1.
Bind off knitwise on next row. ■

Plush Scarf

Design by George Shaheen

Big needles and chenille yarn create
this cozy scarf with extra-lush warmth.

Skill Level ◼◼◼◻ INTERMEDIATE

Finished Size
Approx 6½ x 64 inches

Materials
- Bulky weight yarn (108 yds/6 oz per skein): 12 oz gold
- Bulky weight chenille yarn (75 yds per skein): 150 yds jade print
- Size 11 (8mm) circular knitting needle or size needed to obtain gauge

Gauge
13 sts = 6½ inches in pat
Gauge is not critical to this project.

Pattern Notes
Circular needle is used to accommodate pattern. Work back and forth in rows; do not join.

Scarf is reversible.

Sl all sts as if to purl with yarn in back.

Scarf
With A, cast on 13 sts.

Row 1: Yo, sl 1, [k1, yo, sl 1] 6 times. (20 sts)

Row 2: K2tog, [yo, sl 1, k2tog] 6 times. (19 sts)

Row 3: Yo, sl 1, [k2tog, yo, sl 1] 6 times. (20 sts)

Row 4: K2tog, [yo, sl 1, k2tog] 6 times. (19 sts)

Rows 5–12: [Rep Rows 3 and 4] 4 times.

Row 13: With B, yo, sl 1, [k2tog, yo, sl 1] 6 times. (20 sts)

Slide all sts to other end of needle.

Row 14: With A, p2tog, [yo, sl 1, p2tog] 6 times. (19 sts)

Row 15: With B, yo, sl 1, [p2tog, yo, sl 1] 6 times. (20 sts)

Slide all sts to other end of needle.

Row 16: With A, k2tog, [yo, sl 1, k2tog] 6 times. (19 sts)

Rep Rows 13–16 until piece measures approx 61 inches, ending with Row 16. Cut B.

Next 12 rows: With A, [rep Rows 3 and 4] 6 times.

Bind off loosely in pat as follows: P1, [k2tog, p1] 6 times. ■

Comfy Ruby
Scarf

Design from Caron International

This soft, luscious scarf will keep you warm when the temperature drops.

Skill Level ◼◼◻◻ EASY

Finished Size
Approx 5 x 50 inches

Materials
- Medium weight yarn (100 yds/ 70.9g per skein): 2 skeins ruby
- Size 10½ (6.5mm) needles

Gauge
16 sts = 4 inches/10cm in pat
Gauge is not critical to this project.

Special Abbreviation
KW2 (Knit Wrapping Twice): Knit next st wrapping yarn twice around needle.

Scarf
Cast on 21 sts.
Knit 5 rows.

Beg pat
Row 1: K1, *KW2; rep from * to last st, k1.
Row 2: Knit across, dropping 2nd wrap of each st.
Rows 3 and 4: Knit.
Rep Rows 1–4 for pat until scarf measures approx 50 inches or desired length.
Knit 5 rows.
Bind off all sts. ◼

Warm Ribbed Scarf

Design by Kathy Wesley

This super simple scarf blends wearability and warmth.

Skill Level ◧■◻◻ EASY

Finished Size
Approx 4 x 62 inches
(excluding fringe)

Materials

- Sport weight yarn
  (108 yds/100g
  per ball):
  1 ball chocolate brown
- Size 8 (5mm) needles or size
  needed to obtain gauge
- Size H/8 (5mm) crochet hook

Gauge
24 sts = 4 inches/10cm in pat
Gauge is not critical to this project.

Scarf
Cast on 25 sts.
Row 1 (RS): K1, *yo, k2tog, p1, k1; rep from * across.
Row 2: P1, *yo, p2tog, k1, p1; rep from * across.
   Rep Rows 1 and 2 until piece measures approx 62 inches.
   Bind off in k1, p1 ribbing.

Finishing
Make Single Knot Fringe referring to page 17. Cut 10-inch strands of yarn, use 2 strands for each knot. Tie knots in each rib across.
   Rep on opposite end. ∎

Holiday
Warmer

Design by Svetlana Avrakh

Cheery holiday colors and an interesting cable pattern combine for a stylish scarf.

Skill Level ■■■◻ INTERMEDIATE

Finished Size
Approx 7 x 54 inches

Materials
- Worsted weight yarn (210 yds/100g per skein): 1 skein each barn red (MC), gray heather (A), white (B), sage green (C)
- Size 5 (3.75mm) straight and circular needles
- Size 7 (4.5mm) needles or size needed to obtain gauge
- Cable needle
- Tapestry needle

Gauge
20 sts and 26 rows = 4 inches/ 10cm in St st with larger needles To save time, take time to check gauge.

Special Abbreviations
T3B (Twist 3 Back): Sl next st to cn, and hold in back, k2, p1 from cn.
T3F (Twist 3 Front): Sl next 2 sts to cn and hold in front, p1, k2 from cn.
C4B (Cable 4 Back): Sl next 2 sts to cn and hold in back, k2, k2 from cn.

C4F (Cable 4 Front): Sl next 2 sts to cn and hold in front, k2, k2 from cn.
T4B (Twist 4 Back): Sl next 2 sts to cn and hold in back, k2, p2 from cn.
T4F (Twist 4 Front): Sl next 2 sts to cn and hold in front, p2, k2 from cn.

Scarf
With smaller needles and MC, cast on 25 sts.
Row 1 (RS): K1, *p1, k1; rep from * across.
Rows 2–7: Rep Row 1 for seed st pat, inc 1 st at center of last row. (26 sts)
Change to larger needles and work as follows:
Row 1 (RS): Purl.
Row 2: Knit.
Row 3 (inc row): P12, [p1, k1] in next st, [k1, p1] in next st, p12. (28 sts)
Row 4 (inc row): K12, [k1, p1] in next st, p2, [p1, k1] in next st, k12. (30 sts)
Row 5: P11, T4B, T4F, p11.
Row 6 and all WS rows not given: Knit the knit sts and purl the purl sts.
Row 7: P10, T3B, p4, T3F, p10.

Row 9: P10, k2, p6, k2, p10.
Row 11: P10, T3F, p4, T3B, p10.
Row 13 (inc row): P4, [p1, k1] in next st, [k1, p1] in next st, p5, T3F, p2, T3B, p5, [p1, k1] in next st, [k1, p1] in next st, p4. (34 sts)
Row 14 (inc row): K4, [k1, p1] in next st, p2, [p1, k1] in next st, k6, p2, k2, p2, k6, [k1, p1] in next st, p2, [p1, k1] in next st, k4. (38 sts)
Row 15: P3, T4B, T4F, p5, T3F, T3B, p5, T4B, T4F, p3.
Row 17: P3, k2, p4, T4F, p4, C4B, p4, T4B, p4, k2, p3.
Row 19: P3, T4F, p4, [T4F, T4B] twice, p4, T4B, p3.
Row 21: P5, T4F, p4, [C4F, p4] twice, T4B, p5.
Row 23: P7, [T4F, T4B] 3 times, p7.
Row 25: P9, [C4B, p4] 3 times, p5.
Row 27: P7, [T4B, T4F] 3 times, p7.
Row 29: P5, T4B, [p4, C4F] twice, p4, T4F, p5.
Row 31: P3, T4B, p4, [T4B, T4F] twice, p4, T4F, p3.
Row 33: P3, k2, p4, T4B, p4, C4B, p4, T4F, p4, k2, p3.
Row 35: P3, T4F, T4B, p5, T3B, T3F, p5, T4F, T4B, p3.
Row 37 (dec row): P5, ssk, k2tog, p6, T3B, p2, T3F, p6, ssk, k2tog, p5. (34 sts)
Row 38 (dec row): K4, [k2tog]

twice, k5, p2, k4, p2, k5, [k2tog] twice, k4. (30 sts)

Row 39: P10, T3B, p4, T3F, p10.

Row 41: P10, T3F, p4, T3B, p10.

Row 43: P11, T4F, T4B, p11.

Row 45 (dec row): P13, ssk, k2tog, p13. (28 sts)

Row 46 (dec row): K12, [k2tog] twice, k12. (26 sts)

Row 47: Purl.

Row 48: Knit.

Continue in St st as follows:

With A, work 4 rows.

With C, work 4 rows.

With B, work 4 rows.

With MC, work 4 rows.

Last 16 rows form stripe pat. Continue in stripe pat until work measures approximately 47 inches from beg, ending with C.

Next row (RS): With MC, knit. Beg with WS facing, work Rows 2–48 as above.

Change to smaller needles and work 6 rows in seed st, dec 1 st at center of first row. Bind off all sts in pat.

Side Edging

With circular needle and MC, RS facing, pick up and knit 257 sts along side of scarf. Work 6 rows in seed st. Bind off all sts in pat. Rep for other side. ∎

Zigzag Scarves

Designs by Patons

Punch up the color and be ready for fun with creatively crooked stripings!

Skill Level ◼◼◻◻ EASY

Finished Size
Adult: Approx 5½ x 64 inches
Child: Approx 5 x 40 inches

Materials
Adult
- Super bulky acrylic blend yarn (86 yds/ 100g per ball): 2 balls peacock (MC), 2 balls multicolor blend (CC)
- Size 15 (10mm) needles or size needed to obtain gauge

Child
- Sport weight acrylic yarn (133 yds/50g per ball): 1 ball mango (MC), 1 ball Kool-Aid variegated (CC)
- Size 7 (4.5mm) needles or size needed to obtain gauge

Adult Scarf

Gauge
9 sts and 16 rows = 4 inches/ 10cm in garter st
To save time, take time to check gauge.

Pattern Note
Slip all stitches as to purl.
With MC, cast on 12 sts.
Row 1: Knit.
Rows 2, 4, 6, 8 and 10: Knit.
Row 3: K10, sl next st to RH needle, bring yarn around slipped st to front of work, sl st back to LH needle (wrap made), turn, leaving rem sts unworked.
Row 5: K8, wrap and turn, leaving rem sts unworked.
Row 7: K6, wrap and turn, leaving rem sts unworked.
Row 9: K4, wrap and turn, leaving rem sts unworked.
Row 11: K2, wrap and turn, leaving rem sts unworked.
Rows 12–14: Knit. Cut yarn at end of Row 14.
 With CC, work Rows 1–14. Cut yarn at end of Row 14.
 With MC, work Rows 1–13. Cut yarn at end of Row 13.
 With CC, work Rows 1–14. Cut yarn at end of Row 14.
 With MC, work Rows 1–14. Cut yarn at end of Row 14.
 With CC, work Rows 1–13. Cut yarn at end of Row 13.
 These 82 rows complete 1 full wave.

[Rep wave pat] 4 times more for a total of 5 waves.
 Bind off all sts.

Pompom
Make 2 of each with MC and CC
Make 3-inch pompoms, following instructions on page 17. Attach CC pompoms to cast-on end and MC pompoms to bound-off end of scarf at corners.

Child Scarf

Gauge
18 sts and 40 rows = 4 inches/ 10cm in garter st
To save time, take time to check gauge.

Pattern Note
Slip all stitches as to purl.
With MC, cast on 24 sts.
Row 1: Knit.
Row 2, 4, 6, 8, 10, 12 and 14: Knit.
Row 3: K21, sl next st to RH needle, bring yarn around slipped st to front of work, sl st back to LH needle (wrap made), turn, leaving rem sts unworked.
Row 5: K18, wrap and turn,

leaving rem sts unworked.

Row 7: K15, wrap and turn, leaving rem sts unworked.

Row 9: K12, wrap and turn, leaving rem sts unworked.

Row 11: K9, wrap and turn, leaving rem sts unworked.

Row 13: K6, wrap and turn, leaving rem sts unworked.

Row 15: K3, wrap and turn, leaving rem sts unworked.

Rows 16–18: Knit. Cut yarn at end of Row 18.

With CC, [work Rows 1–18] once. Cut yarn at end of Row 18.

With MC, [work Rows 1–17] once. Cut yarn at end of Row 17.

With CC, [work Rows 1–18] once. Cut yarn at end of Row 18.

With MC, [work Rows 1–18] once. Cut yarn at end of Row 18.

With CC, [work Rows 1–17] once. Cut yarn at end of Row 17.

These 106 rows complete 1 full wave. [Rep wave pat] 5 times more for a total of 6 waves.

Bind off all sts.

Pompom
Make 2 of each with MC and CC

Make 2-inch pompoms, following instructions on page 17. Attach CC pompoms to cast-on end and MC pompoms to bound-off end of scarf at corners. ∎

Cozy Amethyst Scarf

Design from Caron International

This warm and cozy scarf will make even a chilly day seem bright.

Skill Level ◖■■◻◻◻ EASY

Finished Size
Approx 9 x 48 inches

Materials
- Medium weight yarn (100 yds/ 70.9g per skein): 3 skeins amethyst
- Size 13 (9mm) needles

Gauge
12 sts and 16 rows = 4 inches/10cm
Gauge is not critical to this project.

Scarf
Cast on 35 sts.
Row 1: Knit.
Row 2: K2, *k1, p1; rep from * to last 3 sts, k3.
Row 3: K2, *p1, k1; rep from * to last 3 sts, p1, k2.
Rep Rows 2 and 3 until scarf measures approx 48 inches or desired length.
Knit 1 row.
Bind off all sts. ∎

Autumn Lace Scarf

Design by Frances Hughes

Blend delicate lace and autumn hues to make this lovely scarf.

Skill Level ◖■◻◻ EASY

Finished Size
Approx 6½ x 60 inches

Materials
- Bulky weight mohair blend yarn (154 yds/50g per ball): 1 ball autumn
- D.K. weight viscose blend yarn (115 yds/50g per ball): 1 ball brown
- Size 15 (10mm) needles or size needed to obtain gauge
- Tapestry needle

Gauge
10 sts = 4 inches/10cm in pat
Gauge is not critical to this project.

Pattern Note
Scarf is worked with 1 strand of each yarn held tog throughout.

Scarf
Cast on 15 sts, knit 1 row.

Row 1 (RS): K2, *yo, p1, p3tog, p1, yo, k1, rep from * to last st, end k1.

Row 2 and all WS rows: K1, purl to last st, k1.

Row 3: [K3, yo, sl 1, k2tog, psso, yo] twice, k3.

Row 5: K1, p2tog, p1, yo, k1, yo, p1, p3tog, p1, yo, k1, yo, p1, p2tog, k1.

Row 7: K1, k2tog, yo, k3, yo, sl 1, k2tog, psso, yo, k3, yo, ssk, k1.

Row 8: Rep Row 2.

Rep Rows 1–8 until 1 yd of shorter yarn remains or until desired length is reached. Bind off all sts. Wet block and pin to shape, if desired. ∎

Fringed
Scarf

Design by George Shaheen

Stitched with large needles this lightweight scarf delivers top-notch style in a jiffy.

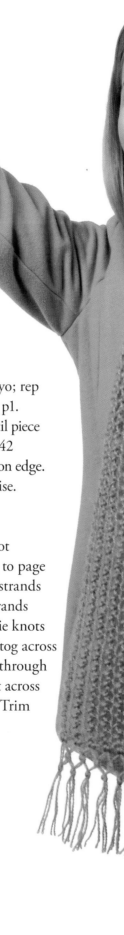

Skill Level ◼◼◻◻◻ EASY

Finished Size
Approx 5 x 42 inches (excluding fringe)

Materials
- Worsted weight brushed acrylic blend yarn (222 yds/2½ oz per ball): 1 ball moss green **[4 MEDIUM]**
- Size 10½ (6.5mm) needles or size needed to obtain gauge

Gauge
12 sts = 4 inches/10cm in pat
Gauge is not critical to this project.

Pattern Note
Scarf is reversible.

Scarf
Cast on 15 sts.
Row 1: *P2tog, yo; rep from * to last st, p1.
   Rep Row 1 until piece measures approx 42 inches from cast-on edge.
   Bind off purlwise.

Fringe
Make Triple Knot Fringe, referring to page 17. Cut 16-inch strands of yarn, use 2 strands for each knot. Tie knots through each p2tog across 1 short end and through each edge purl st across other short end. Trim ends even. ◼

Evening Intrigue Scarf

Design by Sue Childress

This fascinating scarf keeps you warm and adds shine to your style.

Skill Level ◖■◻◻ EASY

Finished Size
Approx 15 x 72 inches

Materials

- Bulky weight metallic novelty yarn (90 yds/50g per ball): 2 balls pink blend
- Bulky weight nylon eyelash yarn (148 yds/50g per ball): 1 ball pink pizzazz
- Size 35 (19mm) needles

5 BULKY

Gauge
6 sts = 4 inches/10cm in garter st with 2 strands held tog
Gauge is not critical to this project.

Scarf
With 1 strand of each yarn held tog throughout, cast on 20 sts.

Knit every row until scarf measures approx 72 inches.

Bind off. ■

Diamond Twist Scarf

Design by Kathy Wesley

This scarf has panache thanks to the fascinating stitch pattern.

Finished Size

Approx 6½ x 52 inches
(excluding fringe)

Materials

- Worsted weight yarn (253 yds/5 oz per skein): 2 skeins claret red
- Size 6 (4mm) circular knitting needle or size needed to obtain gauge

Gauge

10 sts and 14 rows = 2 inches/5cm in St st
To save time, take time to check gauge.

Pattern Note

A chart is included for Rows 1–24 of the pattern for the body of the scarf.

Scarf

Cast on 33 sts.

STITCH KEY
- ☐ K on RS, p on WS
- ⊟ K on WS, p on RS
- ⊿ K2tog
- ⟍ Ssk
- ○ Yo
- ⋀ Sl1, k2tog, psso

Lower border

Row 1 (WS): K1, purl to last st, k1.
Row 2 (RS): K2, [k2tog, yo, k1, yo, ssk, k1] 4 times, end k1.
Rows 3–10: Rep [Rows 1 and 2] 4 times.
Row 11: Rep Row 1.

Body

Row 1 (RS): K2, k2tog, yo, k1, yo, ssk, k7, [yo, ssk] 3 times, k6, k2tog, yo, k1, yo, ssk, k2.
Row 2 and all even-numbered rows: K1, purl to last st, k1.
Row 3: K2, k2tog, yo, k1, yo, ssk, k5, k2tog, yo, k1, [yo, ssk] 3 times, k5, k2tog, yo, k1, yo, ssk, k2.
Row 5: K2, k2tog, yo, k1, yo, ssk, k4, [k2tog, yo] twice, k1, [yo, ssk] 3 times, k4, k2tog, yo, k1, yo, ssk, k2.
Row 7: K2, k2tog, yo, k1, yo, ssk, k3, [k2tog, yo] 3 times, k1, [yo, ssk] 3 times, k3, k2tog, yo, k1, yo, ssk, k2.
Row 9: K2, k2tog, yo, k1, yo, ssk, k2, [k2tog, yo] 3 times, k3, [yo, ssk] 3 times, k2, k2tog, yo, k1, yo, ssk, k2.
Row 11: K2, k2tog, yo, k1, yo, ssk, k1, [k2tog, yo] 3 times, k5, [yo, ssk] 3 times, k1, k2tog, yo, k1, yo, ssk, k2.
Row 13: K2, k2tog, yo, k1, yo, ssk, k1, [yo, ssk] twice, yo, k3, sl 1 as if to knit, k2tog, psso, k3, [yo, k2tog] twice, yo, k1, k2tog, yo, k1, yo, ssk, k2.
Row 15: K2, k2tog, yo, k1, yo, ssk, k2, [yo, ssk] twice, yo, k2, sl 1 as if to knit, k2tog, psso, k2, [yo, k2tog] twice, yo, k2, k2tog, yo, k1, yo, ssk, k2.
Row 17: K2, k2tog, yo, k1, yo, ssk, k3, [yo, ssk] twice, yo, k1, sl 1

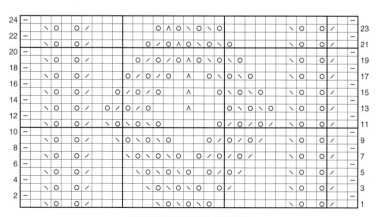

DIAMOND TWIST CHART

as if to knit, k2tog, psso, k1, [yo, k2tog] twice, yo, k3, k2tog, yo, k1, yo, ssk, k2.

Row 19: K2, k2tog, yo, k1, yo, ssk, k4, [yo, ssk] twice, yo, sl 1 as if to knit, k2tog, psso, [yo, k2tog] twice, yo, k4, k2tog, yo, k1, yo, ssk, k2.

Row 21: K2, k2tog, yo, k1, yo, ssk, k5, [yo, ssk] twice, yo, sl 1 as if to knit, k2tog, psso, yo, k2tog, yo, k5, k2tog, yo, k1, yo, ssk, k2.

Row 23: K2, k2tog, yo, k1, yo, ssk, k6, [yo, ssk] twice, yo, sl 1 as if to knit, k2tog, psso, yo, k6, k2tog, yo, k1, yo, ssk, k2.

Row 24: K1, purl to last st, k1.

Rep Rows 1–24 until scarf measures approx 50 inches.

Rep Rows 1 and 2.

Upper border

Row 1 (RS): K2, [k2tog, yo, k1, yo, ssk, k1] 4 times, k1.

Row 2: K1, purl to last st, k1.

Rows 3–10: Rep [Rows 1 and 2] 4 times.

Bind off.

Fringe

Following Fringe instructions on page 17, make Spaghetti Fringe. Cut 6-inch strands. Tie a knot in every st across each short end of scarf. Trim ends even. ■

Cotillion Scarf

Design by George Shaheen

Show off your sparkle with this bright red, fluffy design!

Skill Level ⬛⬛☐☐ EASY

Finished Size
Approx 4½ x 42 inches

Materials

- Worsted weight metallic yarn (115 yds/1¾ oz per ball): 2 balls ruby (A)
- Novelty polyester eyelash yarn (60 yds/1¾ oz per ball): 1 ball red (B)
- Size 15 (10mm) needles
- Size 17 (12.75mm) needles or size needed to obtain gauge

Gauge
12½ sts = 4 inches/10cm in pat with larger needles and 1 strand of each yarn held tog
Gauge is not critical to this project.

Pattern Notes
Scarf ends are worked with 2 strands of metallic yarn held tog; center portion is worked with 1 strand of each yarn held tog.
Scarf is reversible.

Scarf
With smaller needles and 2 strands of A held tog, cast on 14 sts.
Row 1: K2, [p2, k2] 3 times.
Row 2: P2, [k2, p2] 3 times.
Rep Rows 1 and 2 until piece measures approx 4 inches. Cut 1 strand of A, attach 1 strand of B. Change to larger needles.

With 1 strand of each yarn held tog, continue in established pat until scarf measures approx 38 inches. Cut B, attach 1 strand of A. Change to smaller needles.

With 2 strands of A held tog, continue in pat until scarf measures 42 inches.
Bind off in pat.

Scarf Rings
Make 2
With smaller needles and 2 strands of A held tog, cast on 4 sts.
Row 1 (RS): P1, k2, p1.
Row 2: K1, p2, k1.
Rows 3–8: [Rep Rows 1 and 2] 3 times more.
Bind off all sts.

Finishing
Step 1: For scarf ring, with RS facing, sew bound-off edge to cast-on edge to form ring. Rep for 2nd ring.
Step 2: Slide end of scarf through scarf ring to first row of B, tack in place to hold. Rep with 2nd ring on opposite end of scarf. ■

Shimmering Scarf

Design by Kathy Sasser

It's fast, easy and oh, so tantalizing—this sparkly evening scarf turns a simple outfit into a dazzler!

Skill Level ◼◻◻ EASY

Finished Size
Approx 4 x 62 inches

Materials
- D.K. weight novelty yarn (148 yds/50g per skein): 2 skeins mulberry

  3 LIGHT
- Size 9 (5.5mm) double-pointed needles or size needed to obtain gauge

Gauge
Approx 24 sts and 25 rows = 4 inches/10cm in St st
Gauge is not critical to this project.

Scarf
First fringe
Beg with longest fringe, cast on 6 sts and work in St st until piece measures 8½ inches, ending with a WS row.

Cut yarn and set needle aside, with RS facing.

Second fringe
Work as first fringe until piece measures 7 inches, ending with a WS row.

Cut yarn and transfer these sts onto first needle on left side of first piece of fringe. Make sure RS is facing on both pieces.

Third fringe
Work as first fringe until piece measures 5½ inches, ending with a WS row.

Cut yarn and transfer sts onto first needle as before.

Fourth fringe
Work as first fringe until piece measures 4 inches, ending with a WS row.

Cut yarn and transfer sts onto first needle as before.

Body
With RS facing, attach yarn and knit across all 24 sts, placing marker at beg of this row. Continue in St st until piece measures 45 inches, or desired length from marker, ending with a WS row.

Bottom Fringe
Work back and forth in St st across first 6 sts on needle, until piece measures 8½ inches. Bind off.

With RS facing, attach yarn and work back and forth in St st across next 6 sts until piece measures 7 inches. Bind off.

With RS facing, attach yarn and work back and forth in St st across next 6 sts until piece

measures 5½ inches. Bind off.

With RS facing, attach yarn and work back and forth in St st across last 6 sts until piece measures 4 inches.

Bind off all sts. ◼

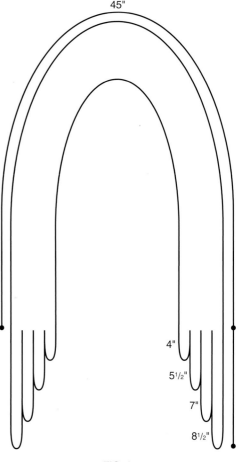

45"

4"

5½"

7"

8½"

FIG. 1

Glitzy Scarf

Design by E.J. Slayton

Knit this soft and simple scarf for a quick last-minute gift.

Skill Level ■■□□ EASY

Finished Size
Approx 37 x 15 inches

Materials

- Eyelash yarn (72 yds/50g per ball): 2 balls summer fiesta
- Size 10½ (7mm) needles
- Stitch marker
- Tapestry needle

Gauge
14 sts = 4 inches/10cm in garter st
Gauge is not critical to this project.

Special Abbreviation
M1 (Make 1): Inc by making a backward lp over the right needle. On next row, be sure to knit so lp remains twisted.

Pattern Note
On all odd-numbered rows, sl first 2 sts purlwise with yarn in front, take yarn to back between needles.

Scarf
Cast on 4 sts.

Row 1: Sl 2, pm, k1, M1, k1.
Row 2: Knit.
Row 3: Sl 2, knit to last st, M1, k1.
Rep Rows 2 and 3 until there are 45 sts, ending with Row 2.

Dec rows
Row 1: Knit.
Row 2: Sl 2, knit to last 3 sts, end k2tog, k1.
Rep 2 dec rows until 4

sts remain, ending with Row 2.
Next row: Sl 2, k2tog, p2sso. Fasten off. ■

Sparkle Scarf

Design by Diane Zangl

A small project with lots of pizzazz, this versatile scarf is a perfect introduction to lace knitting for the beginner.

Skill Level ■■□□ EASY

Finished Size

18 inches long x 40 inches wide at top

Materials

- Metallic worsted weight yarn (85 yds/25g per ball): 3 balls silver
- Size 8 (5mm) needles or size needed to obtain gauge
- Tapestry needle

Gauge

8 sts and 12 rows = 4 inches/10cm in pat
To save time, take time to check gauge.

Pattern Notes

Work first 3 and last 3 sts very loose/long to give enough ease to cover vertical spread of lace.

Special Abbreviations

R inc (Right increase): Knit bar of st below, knit st on LH ndl.

L inc (Left increase): Knit next st, knit bar of st below.

Pattern Stitch
Knotted Mesh

Row 1 (RS): K1, R inc, *yo twice, k1; rep from * to last 2 sts, L inc, k1.

Row 2: K3, *k1, knit first yo lp, purl 2nd yo lp, p2sso purl st; rep from * to last 3 sts, k3.

Rep Rows 1 and 2 for pat.

Scarf

Cast on 4 sts. Knit 2 rows.

Set up pat

Next row: K1, R inc, L inc, k1.

Work in Knotted Mesh pat until there are 80 sts on needle, ending with Row 2.

Top Border

Next row (RS): K1, R inc, *yo, k1; rep from * to last 2 sts, L inc, kl. Knit 2 rows. Bind off loosely. ∎

Faux Fur
Collar & Cuffs

Design by Ellen Edwards Drechsler

Start the new year off in style when you make an easy fur collar and cuff set for your winter coat or jacket.

Skill Level ◼◼◻◻ EASY

Finished Size
Collar: Approx 35 x 14 inches
Cuffs: Approx 5 inches wide

Materials
Collar
- Polyester eyelash yarn (60 yds/1.75 oz per skein): 2 skeins each black, copper, chocolate
- Size 11 (8mm) needles or size needed to obtain gauge
- Tapestry needle

Cuffs
- Polyester eyelash yarn (60 yds/1.75 oz per skein): 2 skeins each black, copper, chocolate
- Size 11 (8mm) needles or size needed to obtain gauge
- Tapestry needle
- 1 package black beading elastic cord

Gauge
8 sts = 4 inches/10cm in garter st
To save time, take time to check gauge.

Pattern Notes
Project is worked with 1 strand of each color held tog.

Wrap collar around neck of coat, secure by putting coat button through yo's at edge.

Use 1 skein of each color for each cuff.

Collar
Using 1 strand of each color, cast on 4 sts.
Row 1: K2, yo, knit to end.

Rep Row 1, attaching new skein as needed, until there is just enough yarn left to bind off.

Bind off all sts loosely.

Cuffs
Using 1 strand of each color, cast on 30 sts.

Work in garter st until cuff is approx 5 inches wide, leaving enough yarn to bind off.

Bind off all sts.

Sew shorter (selvage) edges tog to form cuff. With tapestry needle, run a strand of elastic around each edge of cuff. Try cuffs on, adjust elastic to fit and fasten off securely. ◼

Chic Cowl
& Cuffs
Design from Bernat Yarns

All ages will love wearing
these fun accessories.

Skill Level ◼☐☐☐ BEGINNER

Finished Size
Cowl: Approx 20 inches around x
9 inches high
Cuffs: Approx 7 inches around

Materials
• Super bulky nylon
  eyelash yarn (77
  yds/50g per ball): 2 balls
  purple flash
• Size 11 (8mm) needles or size
  needed to obtain gauge

6 SUPER BULKY

Gauge
11 sts and 14 rows = 4 inches/
10cm in St st
Gauge is not critical to this project.

Cowl
Cast on 54 sts.
   Work in St st until piece measures
9 inches.
   Bind off all sts.
   Sew side edges tog.

Cuffs
Cast on 18 sts.
   Work in St st until work
measures 3½ inches, ending with a
purl row.
   Bind off all sts.
   Sew side edges tog. ◼

Ready
for Winter

Design by Lorna Miser

Using roving makes this set super quick and easy.

Skill Level ◼️◼️◻️◻️ EASY

Materials
- Wool top or roving for hand-spinning: 1 bundle (approx10 oz) will make both a headband and scarf, variegated
- 2 yards of any bulky yarn for temporary cast on
- Size 19 (15mm) needles or size needed to obtain gauge
- Tapestry needle

Headband

Using scrap yarn, cast on 4 very loose sts over both needles. Drop scrap yarn and beg knitting with wool top. Once knit, sts hold fibers well and it is not nearly as delicate as yarn alone is.

Work in St st for about 20 inches. Break yarn, leaving a 12-inch end. Remove scrap yarn. Weave or sew last row of sts to bottom of first row. To hide ends, split each tail in half and bury in opposite directions.

Scarf

Cast on loosely 6 sts. Work in St st for desired length. Bind off.

Knit roving responds well to hot steam for blocking. This flattens St st curl and sets sts. Very gentle hand washing in a sink is recommended. With time and wear, these garments will gain a soft, fuzzy haze. ◼️

Ski Band
Stripes

Design by Virginia Vaughn

Keep your ears toasty warm on the slopes with this snazzy ski band.

Skill Level ◼◼◼◻ INTERMEDIATE

Finished Size
3½ inches wide, 22-inch circumference

Materials
- Acrylic chunky weight yarn (42 yds/39m per ball): 1 ball green (A)
- Chunky weight wool yarn (60 yds/55m per ball): 1 ball white (B)
- Size 10½ (6.5mm) needles or size needed to obtain gauge
- Tapestry needle

5 BULKY

Gauge
5 sts and 6 rnds = 2 inches/5cm in St st
To save time, take time to check gauge.

Pattern Notes
1 skein of each yarn will make 2 ski bands.

Size may be changed by casting on more or fewer sts in 2-st increments to match the pat rep. For a narrower band (approximately 3 inches) omit 1 row of B on each side of band.

Ski Band
With A, cast on 55 sts using a long tail cast on. Turn work so the "purl bump" is toward outside (which will be RS of ski band) and yarn is attached on LH needle. Join by sl 1 st from RH needle to LH needle, then knit first 2 sts tog. (54 sts)
With A, knit 1 row.
Rnds 1–3: With B, knit.
Rnd 4: *K1 A, k1 B; rep from * around.
Rnd 5: With A, knit.
Rnd 6: *K1 A, K1 B; rep from * around.
Rnds 7–9: With B, knit.
Rnd 10: With A, knit.
Bind off in purl, creating a garter ridge. ■

School Colors

Design by Uyvonne Bigham

Scarf & Hat

Knitted in the round, this great scarf has an all-American look perfect for guys and gals.

Skill Level ■■■□ INTERMEDIATE

Finished Size
Scarf: Approx 4 x 60 inches (excluding tassels)
Hat Circumference: Approx 19 inches

Materials
- Worsted weight yarn (220 yds/100g per ball): 2 balls blue (MC), 1 ball off-white (CC) **4 MEDIUM**
- Size 8 (5mm) double-pointed needles or size needed to obtain gauge
- Stitch marker
- 6-inch-wide piece of cardboard

Gauge
17 sts and 26 rnds = 4 inches/ 10cm in St st
To save time, take time to check gauge.

Pattern Note
Yarn is sufficient for both scarf and hat.

Scarf
With MC, cast on 40 sts. Join without twisting and place marker at beg of rnd.

Knit with MC until work measures 3 inches from beg. Change to CC and work 4 rnds. Change to MC and work 24 rnds. Change to CC and work 4 rnds.

Change to MC and work even until scarf measures approx 55 inches from beg.

Change to CC and work 4 rnds. Change to MC and work 24 rnds. Change to CC and work 4 rnds.

Change to MC and work even until scarf measures 60 inches from beg.

Cut yarn leaving about a 12-inch tail.

Weave in all ends except tail and cast-on edge.

Finishing
Using tail from end of scarf, draw yarn through open sts. Pull tightly and secure. Rep for cast-on edge. Run yarn through all sts and draw up tightly.

Tassels
Make 2
Wrap yarn around a 6-inch-wide piece of cardboard. Thread a strand of yarn into yarn needle and insert it under strands along edge of cardboard. Tie at top, leaving a long end to wrap around tassel. Cut strands at opposite edge of cardboard. Wrap tassel about 1 inch below top, fasten securely.

Attach a tassel to beg and end of scarf.

Hat
With MC, cast on 80 sts. Join without twisting and place marker at beg of rnd.

Work 24 rnds. Change to CC and work 4 rnds. Change to MC and work 12 rnds. Change to CC and work 4 rnds. Change to MC and work even until hat measures 10 inches from beg.

Shape top
Rnd 1: *K8, k2tog; rep from * around. (72 sts)
Rnd 2 and all even rnds: Knit.
Rnd 3: *K7, k2tog; rep from * around. (64 sts)
Rnd 5: *K6, k2tog; rep from * around. (56 sts)

Rnd 7: *K5, k2tog; rep from * around. (48 sts)

Rnd 9: *K4, k2tog; rep from * around. (40 sts)

Rnd 11: *K3, k2tog; rep from * around. (32 sts)

Rnd 13: *K2, k2tog; rep from * around. (24 sts)

Rnd 15: *K1, k2tog; rep from * around. (16 sts)

Rnd 17: *K2tog; rep from * around. (8 sts)

Cut yarn leaving a 12-inch tail. Thread tail into a yarn needle and draw through all sts. Secure tightly.

Roll up cast-on edge. ■

Big Needle Winter Set

Design by Diane Zangl

Big needles, chunky yarn and a broken rib pattern are the ingredients for a warm and quick-to-knit winter set.

Skill Level ◼◻◻ EASY

Finished Sizes

Scarf: Approx 8 x 45 inches (without tassels)

Hat: One size fits most adults

Materials

- Chunky weight wool/acrylic blend yarn (43 yds/100g per ball): 5 balls aqua for scarf, 3 balls aqua for hat
- Size 10 (6mm) needles or size needed to obtain gauge
- Tapestry needle
- 6-inch piece of cardboard

Gauge

14 sts and 16 rows = 4 inches/ 10cm in Broken Rib pat

To save time, take time to check gauge.

Pattern Stitches

A. 1/1 Rib

Row 1 (RS): K1, *p1, k1; rep from * across.

Row 2: P1, *k1, p1; rep from * across.

Rep Rows 1 and 2 for pat.

B. Broken Rib

Row 1 (RS): K1, *p1, k1; rep from * across.

Row 2: Purl.

Rep Rows 1 and 2 for pat.

Pattern Notes

Each end is folded under to form points, which may be used as mini pockets.

Sl first st of every WS row purlwise wyif; sl first st of all RS rows knitwise wyib.

Scarf

Cast on 23 sts. Beg with Row 2, work even in Pat B for 46 inches.

Bind off all sts.

Fold bound-off edge in half and sew tog to form a point. Rep for cast-on edge.

Tassel

Make 2 tassels as for hat and sew 1 to each end.

Hat

Cast on 61 sts. Work even in Pat A for 1 inch, inc 8 sts evenly on last WS row. (69 sts)

Change to Pat B and work even until hat measures 7 inches, ending with a WS row.

Shape top

Row 1 (RS): K1, *p2tog, k2tog; rep from * across. (35 sts)

Row 2: Purl.

Row 3: Rep Row 1. (18 sts)

Row 4: Purl.

Row 5: K1, [k2tog] to last st, k1. (10 sts)

Cut yarn, leaving an 18-inch end. Draw end through rem sts twice and pull tight.

With same yarn, sew back seam.

Tassel

Make 1

Cut 2 (10-inch) strands of yarn and set aside.

Wrap yarn around cardboard 12 times.

Tie 1 end with a reserved strand. Cut opposite end.

Using 2nd reserved strand, tie tassel 1 inch below first tie. Bury ends in tassel. ◼

A Touch of Color
Hat & Scarf

Designs by Virginia Vaughn

Use circular needles to knit this warm and cozy hat and scarf.

Skill Level ◼◼◻◻ EASY

Finished Sizes
Hat: Approx 22-inch circumference
Scarf: 6 x 56 inches (excluding fringe)

Materials
• Mohair/wool chunky weight yarn (125 yds/4 oz per skein): 2 skeins deep charcoal (A)
• Alpaca Boucle yarn (115 yds/1.75 oz per skein): 1 skein variegated cranberry (B)
• Size 10½ (6.5mm) double-pointed and 16- and 24-inch circular needles or size needed to obtain gauge
• Tapestry needle
• Stitch marker

Gauge
12 sts and 16 rnds = 4 inches/ 10cm in St st with mohair/wool To save time, take time to check gauge.

Pattern Notes
Scarf is knit lengthwise, so adjust length by casting on fewer or more sts.

When changing yarn, leave a length of yarn for fringe as desired. Sample fringe is 5 inches.

Scarf
With A, cast on 168 sts.
Knit 4 rows with A.
Knit 2 rows with B.
Knit 6 rows with A.
[Knit 1 row B, knit 1 row A] 4 times.
Knit 1 row B.
Knit 5 rows A.
Knit 2 rows B.
Knit 4 rows A.
Bind off with A.

Add fringe or weave in ends. To add fringe, cut 12-inch lengths of yarn and add to ends of scarf, combining with previously cut ends. Trim even to desired length.

Hat
With circular needle and A, cast on 65 sts. Join without twisting, place marker at beg of rnd.
Rnds 1–5: Knit.
Rnd 6: With B, purl.
Rnd 7: With A, knit.
Rnds 8–15: Rep [Rnds 6 and 7] 4 times.
Cut B and knit every rnd with A until piece measures 6 inches.

Shape top
Rnd 1: [K11, k2tog] 5 times. (60 sts)
Rnd 2: [K10, k2tog] 5 times. (55 sts)
Rnd 3: [K9, k2tog] 5 times. (50 sts)
Continue to dec in this manner until 10 sts rem.
Last rnd: [K2tog] around. (5 sts)
Cut yarn, run through rem sts and fasten off securely. ◼

Quick & Easy
Roll-Brim Hat

Design by Patsy J. Leatherbury

Looking for a stylish gift? You can sit back and enjoy knitting this warm and comfy hat.

Skill Level ■■■□ INTERMEDIATE

Size
Woman's medium/large
One size fits most.

Finished Measurement
Circumference: Approx 20½ inches

Materials
- Bulky weight yarn (110 yds/50g per ball): 2 balls ocean blue variegated
- Size 8 (5mm) double-pointed and 16-inch circular needles or size needed to obtain gauge
- Stitch marker

Gauge
14 sts and 19 rnds = 4 inches/10cm in St st
To save time, take time to check gauge.

Pattern Notes
To join before beginning first round, slip first stitch of round to right needle, pass last stitch of round over first st and onto left needle—first and last stitches have exchanged places. Place marker between stitches to mark beginning of round.

Change to double-pointed needle when hat becomes too small for circular needle.

Hat
Using circular needle, cast on 64 sts. Join without twisting, marking beg of rnd.

Rnds 1–8: Knit.
Rnds 9–12: *K1, p1; rep from * around.
Rnd 13: *K7, [k1, p1] in next st; rep from * around. (72 sts)

Work in St st for 30 rnds or until hat measures 9 inches from beg.

Shape top
Rnd 1: *K7, k2tog; rep from * around. (64 sts)
Rnd 2 and all even rnds: Knit.
Rnd 3: *K6, k2tog; rep from * around. (56 sts)
Rnd 5: *K5, k2tog; rep from * around. (48 sts)
Rnd 7: *K4, k2tog; rep from * around. (40 sts)
Rnd 9: *K3, k2tog; rep from * around. (32 sts)
Rnd 11: *K2, k2tog; rep from * around. (24 sts)
Rnd 13: *K1, k2tog; rep from * around. (16 sts)
Rnd 15: [K2tog] 8 times. (8 sts)

Cut yarn, leaving a 6-inch tail. Weave yarn through sts, pull tight and fasten off securely. ■

Funky Hemmed Hat

Design by Virginia Vaughn

Sized for a loose fit, the hemmed bottom of this hat provides extra warmth.

Skill Level ◼◼◻◻ EASY

Size
Woman's medium

Materials
- Bulky weight wool yarn (110 yds/100g per skein): 1 skein onyx (A)
- Bulky weight novelty yarn (44 yds/50g per skein): 1 skein variegated (B)
- Size 10½ (6.5mm) double-pointed and 16-inch circular needles or size needed to obtain gauge
- Stitch markers
- Tapestry needle

Gauge
12 sts = 4 inches/10cm in St st with A
To save time, take time to check gauge.

Pattern Notes
Hat has a hemmed bottom for extra warmth and comfort around ears. For less bulk at hem, use open or provisional cast on, then knit hem and hat sts tog. If you are not familiar with this technique, you may use any cast on and loosely sew hem in place when hat is completed.

To join hem when using open cast on, sl sts from auxiliary yarn to spare needle. Fold cuff in half with WS of fabric tog, *knit first st on front and back needles tog, rep from * around.

It is not necessary to cut strands between rnds. Carry colors loosely up inside of hat.

Hat can be made smaller by using a smaller needle. A gauge of 14 sts = 4 inches will make a hat circumference of approx 20½ inches.

Hat
Using circular needle and A, cast on 72 sts. Join without twisting and work in St st for 5 inches. If using open cast on, join hem at this point, do not cut A.

Beg pat
Rnds 1 and 2: With B, purl.
Rnds 3 and 4: With A, knit.
Rep Rnds 1–4 until hat measures 6 inches from fold, or 8½ inches from beg.

Shape top
Maintain established pat, and change to dpn as needed.
Rnd 1: [K10, k2tog, pm] 6 times.
Rnd 2: [Knit to 2 sts before marker, k2tog] 6 times.
Rep Rnd 2 until 6 sts remain.
Cut yarn and thread end through remaining sts. Pull snug and fasten off securely.
Sew hem loosely in place if needed. ◼

Quick Cozy Hat

Design by Virginia Vaughn

Whimsical hats are riding a wave of popularity today. Use novelty yarn to add pizzazz to a simple stockinette stitch hat.

Skill Level ◖■□□ EASY

Size

Woman's medium (large)
Instructions are given for smaller size, with larger size in parentheses. When only 1 number is given, it applies to both sizes.

Materials

- Bulky weight novelty yarn (55 yds/100g per skein): 1 skein green variegated (A)
- Bulky weight wool yarn (110 yds/100g per skein): 1 skein midnight pine (B)
- Size 11 (8mm) double-pointed and 16-inch circular needles or size needed to obtain gauge
- Size 13 (9mm) 16-inch circular needle
- Tapestry needle
- 6-inch-wide piece of cardboard

Gauge

7 sts = 4 inches/10cm in St st with larger needles and A
12 sts = 4 inches/10cm in St st with smaller needles and B
To save time, take time to check gauge.

Hat

With A and larger needles, cast on 35 (40) sts. Join without twisting and work in St st until piece measures 3 inches from beg. Cut A. Change to smaller needles, attach B and inc 25 sts evenly around. (60, 65 sts)
Work in B for 4 inches.

Shape top

Rnd 1: [K10 (11), k2tog] 5 times.
Rnd 2: [K9 (10), k2tog] 5 times.
Rnd 3: [K8 (9), k2tog] 5 times.

Continue to dec in this manner, having 1 less st between dec every rnd until 10 sts remain.
Next rnd: K2tog around.
Cut yarn, leaving a 12-inch end. Thread yarn through sts, pull snug and fasten off securely. Leave end to attach tassel.

Tassel

Wrap A 6 times around cardboard. Pinch center, wrap tightly with yarn and fasten securely to top of hat. ∎

Warm & Toasty Stocking Cap

Design by Lois S. Young

For rustic country winters or urban environments, even preppies can stay warm in this beautifully patterned stocking cap.

Skill Level ◼◼◼◻ INTERMEDIATE

Size
Woman's medium
One size fits most

Finished Measurement
Circumference: Approx 21 inches

Materials
- Sport weight wool yarn (184 yds/1¾ oz per skein): 1 skein each medium brown (MC), natural (A), light moss (B)
- Size 5 (3.75mm) set of double-pointed and 16-inch circular needles or size needed to obtain gauge
- Small piece of cardboard 2 inches wide for making pompom
- Stitch markers

Gauge
24 sts and 30 rnds = 4 inches/ 10cm in St st
To save time, take time to check gauge.

Pattern Notes
Hat stretches so one size fits most.

Change to double-pointed needles when hat becomes too small for circular needle.

Hat
With circular needle and MC, cast on 120 sts. Join without twisting, marking beg of rnd.

Border
Work 8 rnds of k1, p1 ribbing.

Body
Work [Rnds 1–14 of chart] 3 times. On last Rnd 14, place markers every 15 sts to divide hat into eighths.

Shape top
Continue in established pat, dec on Rnds 1 and 8 as follows: *Work to 2 sts before marker, k2tog, rep from * around.

When 16 sts rem, work 1 rnd of k2tog in MC. Break yarn, leaving a 6-inch end. Pull end through all sts, fasten off. Block.

Pompom
For Instructions on making a pompom, see page 17. Make pompom with B and shake to fluff. Trim to a spherical shape.

Pull ends from ties to inside of hat, tie in knot. Do not weave in ends if you want to remove pompom when washing hat. ■

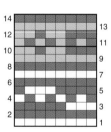

COLOR KEY
◼ MC
◻ A
▨ B

STOCKING CAP CHART

Casual Cables
Ski Tam

Design by Helen Stenborg

Be right in style with this quick-to-knit tam. Knit it to match your favorite ski outfit, and you're ready for the slopes.

Skill Level ◼◼◼◻ INTERMEDIATE

Size
Woman's: one size fits most

Materials
- Bulky weight acrylic yarn (135 yds/3 oz per ball): 1 ball fisherman **5 BULKY**
- Size 6 (4mm) 16-inch circular needle
- Size 8 (5mm) double-pointed and 16-inch circular needles or size needed to obtain gauge
- Stitch markers
- Cable needle
- Tapestry needle

Gauge
12 sts and 20 rnds = 4 inches/10cm in seed st with larger needles
To save time, take time to check gauge.

Special Abbreviation
BC (Back Cross): Sl next 3 sts to cn, hold in back, k3, k3 from cn.

Pattern Stitch
Seed St (on even number of sts)
Rnd 1: *K1, p1; rep from * around.
Rnd 2: *P1, k1; rep from * around.
Rep Rnds 1 and 2 for pat.

With smaller circular needle, cast on 80 sts. Join without twisting, mark beg of rnd and work in k1, p1 ribbing for 2 inches. Change to larger circular needle.

Ski Tam
Rnds 1–9: [Work Seed St across 10 sts, k6] 5 times.
Rnd 10: [Work Seed St across 10 sts, BC] 5 times.
Rep Rnds 1–10 until piece measures 6 inches from beg.

Shape top
Change to dpn, pm every 16 sts (5 sections) and work in St st.
Rnd 1: [K1, k2tog, knit to within 3 sts of next marker, ssk, k1] 5 times.   **Rnd 2:** Knit.
Rep Rnds 1 and 2 until 20 sts rem, then k2tog around.
Divide sts evenly on 2 needles and weave tog.

Top Knot
With larger needles, cast on 28 sts and work in k2, p2 for 12 rows. Cut yarn, leaving an 18-inch end.
Thread end in tapestry needle and run through rem sts, draw up tightly. With same end, seam edges of piece tog, run end through cast-on sts, pull tight and fasten off. Sew to top of tam. Block lightly. ■

Striped Tiptop Hats

Designs by Elizabeth Mattfield

Stripes and felting fun create these unique hats.

Skill Level ◼◼◻◻ EASY

Size

Woman's small (large) Instructions are given for smaller size, with larger size in parentheses. When only 1 number is given, it applies to both sizes.

Materials

- Bulky weight wool yarn (125 yds/4 oz per skein): approx 3 oz total per hat
- Size 13 (9mm) needles
- Tapestry needle

Gauge

In St st, before felting, very loose and airy, final gauge is determined by felting.

Pattern Notes

Basic hat instructions are given first; color instructions follow. Finished size depends a lot on type and color of wool used and how tightly it felts. Easiest way to get correct head size is to dry, and complete felting process over something that is same size you want hat to be.

Hats may also be knitted circular, with 4 dpns and a short circular needle.

Hat

Beg at top, cast on 4 sts.
Row 1 (RS): Inc in each st. (8 sts)
Row 2: Purl.
Row 3: Knit, inc 8 sts evenly.
Row 4: Purl.

Rep Rows 3 and 4 until there are 72 (80) sts, placing incs so they are not directly above previous incs. Purl next RS row (turning ridge). Purl 1 row, dec 4 sts evenly.

Sides

Work 10 rows in St st, dec 4 sts evenly on last row. Work 3 rows garter st. Bind off all sts.

Finishing

Sew seam, then felt. Shape as desired and dry over padded pot or bowl that is desired size.

Shaded Stripes Hat

Red (A), purple (B), blue (C).

With A, cast on and work first 10 rows. Work [1 row B, 1 row A] twice, 2 rows B, 1 row C, 1 row B, 3 rows C (including turning row), [1 row B, 1 row C] twice, 2 rows B, 1 row A, 1 row B, 1 row A, complete hat with A.

COLOR KEY
☐ MC
◇ CC

Rep

HAT CHART

Blue & White Hat

White (MC) and blue (CC).

Cast on with MC and work to turning ridge. Change to CC, work 3 rows CC, then work pat referring to chart. Work last dec row on sides and garter band in CC. ◼

Felting Tip

I usually felt pieces by putting them in the washing machine, hot wash, with minimal water and some real soap. I leave the lid up, and don't let the machine go through the spin part of the cycle and dump all the hot water. I run several cycles that way until the texture looks about right. If the object is small enough, I pull it out of the hot water and dump it in a sink of cold water. Sometimes you can feel it felting in your hands when you do that. If the size or shape is critical, dry the felted object over a form or block, but if it is not critical, putting it in the dryer felts it even firmer.

Candles Triangular Scarf

Design by Sue Childress

Tie your hair back with this lovely scarf
or wear it as a sweater collar.

Skill Level ◼◼◻◻ EASY

Finished Size
Approx 36 x 17 inches (blocked)

Materials

- Ribbon yarn (85 yds/50g per ball): 2 balls light blue
- Size 9 (5.5mm) needles or size needed to obtain gauge
- Tapestry needle

Gauge
16 sts = 4 inches/10cm before blocking

To save time, take time to check gauge.

Scarf
Cast on 3 sts.

Row 1 (RS): Knit.

Row 2: Purl.

Row 3: [K1, yo] twice, k1. (5 sts)

Row 4 and rem even rows through 86: Purl.

Row 5: K1, yo, k3, yo, k1. (7 sts)

Row 7: K1, yo, knit to last st, yo, k1.

Row 8: Rep Row 4.

Rows 9–14: [Rep Rows 7 and 8] 3 times.

Row 15: K1, yo, k4, k2tog, yo, k1, yo, ssk, k4, yo, k1. (17 sts)

Row 17: K1, yo, k4, k2tog, yo, k3, yo, ssk, k4, yo, k1. (19 sts)

Row 19: K1, yo, k4, [k2tog, yo] twice, k1, [yo, ssk] twice, k4, yo, k1. (21 sts)

Row 21: K1, yo, k4, [k2tog, yo] twice, k3, [yo, ssk] twice, k4, yo, k1. (23 sts)

Row 23: K1, yo, k4, [k2tog, yo] 3 times, k1, [yo, ssk] 3 times, k4, yo, k1. (25 sts)

Rows 25–32: [Rep Rows 7 and 8] 4 times. (33 sts)

Row 33: K1, yo, k6, k2tog, yo, k1, yo, ssk, k9, k2tog, yo, k1, yo, ssk, k6, yo, k1. (35 sts)

Row 35: K1, yo, k6, k2tog, yo, k3, yo, ssk, k7, k2tog, yo, k3, yo, ssk, k6, yo, k1. (37 sts)

Row 37: K1, yo, k6, [k2tog, yo] twice, k1, [yo, ssk] twice, k5, [k2tog, yo] twice, k1, [yo, ssk] twice, k6, yo, k1. (39 sts)

Row 39: K1, yo, k6, [k2tog, yo] twice, k3, [yo, ssk] twice, k3, [k2tog, yo] twice, k3, [yo, ssk] twice, k6, yo, k1. (41 sts)

Row 41: K1, yo, k6, [k2tog, yo] 3 times, k1, [yo, ssk] 3 times, k1, [k2tog, yo] 3 times, k1, [yo, ssk] 3 times, k6, yo, k1. (43 sts)

Rows 43–52: [Rep Rows 7 and 8] 3 times. (53 sts)

Row 53: K1, yo, k9, [k2tog, yo, k1, yo, ssk, k9] 3 times, yo, k1. (55 sts)

Row 55: K1, yo, k9, [k2tog, yo, k3, yo, ssk, k7] 3 times, k2, yo, k1. (57 sts)

Row 57: K1, yo, k9, [{k2tog, yo} twice, k1, {yo, ssk} twice, k5] 3 times, k4, yo, k1. (59 sts)

Row 59: K1, yo, k9, [{k2tog, yo} twice, k3, {yo, ssk} twice, k3] 3 times, k6, yo, k1. (61 sts)

Row 61: K1, yo, k9, [{k2tog, yo} 3 times, k1, {yo, ssk} 3 times, k1] 3 times, k8, yo, k1. (63 sts)

Rows 63–78: [Rep Rows 7 and 8] 3 times. (79 sts)

Row 79: K1, yo, knit to last st, yo, k1. (81 sts)

Row 80 (WS): P2, *p2tog, yo; rep from * to last 3 sts, yo, p3.

Rows 81–86: [Rep Rows 7 and 8] 3 times.

Rows 87 and 88: Rep Rows 79 and 80.

Row 89: [K1, yo] twice, knit to last 2 sts, [yo, k1] twice.

Row 90: Purl.

Rows 91–100: [Rep Rows 89 and 90] 5 times.

Bind off all sts in purl.

Wet-block for best results. ◼

Grape Confetti
Designs by Laura Polley
Hat & Scarf Set

Novelty yarn and big needles make this set ultra-quick and lots of fun!

Skill Level ◼◼◻◻ EASY

Finished Size
Child's 2 (4, 6, 8) Instructions are given for smallest size, with larger sizes in parentheses. When only 1 number is given, it applies to all sizes.

Finished Measurements
Hat
Circumference:
19 (20, 21, 22) inches
Total length:
7½ (7½, 8½, 9) inches
Scarf
Width: 6½ (6½, 7½, 7½) inches
Length (without fringe): 38½ (42, 45½, 49) inches

Materials
- Acrylic novelty yarn (38 yds/ 50g per ball): Hat: 1 (2, 2, 2) balls purple rainbow, Scarf: 3 (3, 3, 4) balls purple rainbow
- Size 13 (9mm) double-pointed and straight needles, or size needed to obtain gauge
- Tapestry needle
- Size G/6 crochet hook

Gauge
9½ sts and 18 rnds = 5 inches in St st
8 sts and 18 rows = 4 inches/10cm in ribbing
To save time, take time to check gauge.

Hat
With dpn, very loosely cast on 36 (38, 40, 42) sts.

Divide sts evenly among 3 dpns. Join without twisting, pm between first and last st.

Work in k1, p1 rib for 6 rnds.

Work even in St st until hat measures 3 (3, 3½, 4) inches, dec 0 (2, 0, 2) sts evenly on last rnd. (36, 36, 40, 40 sts)

Shape crown
Rnd 1: *K7 (7, 8, 8), k2tog, rep from * around. (32, 32, 36, 36 sts)
Rnd 2: Knit.
Rnd 3: *K6 (6, 7, 7), k2tog, rep from * around. (28, 28, 32, 32 sts)
Rnd 4: Knit.

Continue to dec every other row as before, having 1 less st between decs each time, until 4 (4, 8, 8) sts rem, end with a dec row.

Sizes 6 & 8 only
Next rnd: K2tog around. (4 sts)

Cut yarn, leaving a 6-inch end.

Draw end through rem sts twice and pull tightly to secure.

Scarf
With straight needles, very loosely cast on 13 (13, 15, 15) sts.
Row 1 (RS): K1, *p1, k1; rep from * across row.
Row 2: P1, *k1, p1; rep from * across row.

Rep Rows 1 and 2 until scarf measures 38½ (42, 45½, 49) inches. Bind off very loosely in rib.

Fringe
Cut strands of yarn, each 6 inches long.

Holding 2 strands tog for each fringe, use crochet hook to attach 1 group of fringe in every other st across cast-on edge of scarf.

Trim fringe even.

Rep along bound-off edge. ∎

Stripy Mohair
Scarf & Hat

Designs by Edie Eckman

Introduce beginners to the joy of knitting with mohair with this spiffy striped set.

Skill Level ■□□□ BEGINNER

Finished Sizes
Scarf: 7 x 60 inches (without fringe)
Hat: 22–23-inch circumference

Materials
- Mohair bulky weight yarn (93 yds/1.5 oz per ball): 2 balls pink (MC), 1 ball each orange (A), purple (B), yellow (C), blue (D), lime (E)
- Size 10½ (7mm) needles or size needed to obtain gauge
- Tapestry needle

Gauge
10½ sts and 18 rows = 4 inches/10cm in striped garter st
To save time, take time to check gauge.

Pattern Note
When working scarf, carry MC up side on contrasting color rows. Do not carry contrasting colors along side.

Stripe Pat
Rows 1 and 2: With A, knit
Rows 3 and 4: With MC, knit.
Rows 5 and 6: With B, knit.
Rows 7 and 8: With MC, knit.
Rows 9 and 10: With C, knit.
Rows 11 and 12: With MC, knit.
Rows 13 and 14: With D, knit.
Row 15 and 16: With MC, knit.
Row 17 and 18: With E, knit.
Rows 19–24: With MC, knit.
Rep Rows 1–24 for Stripe pat.

Scarf
With MC, cast on 18 sts. Knit 5 rows. Work 11 reps of Stripe pat. With MC, bind off loosely.

Fringe
Cut 20 (16-inch) lengths of MC and 10 (16-inch) lengths of each CC. Using 1 strand of each CC and 2 of MC, attach 4-strand fringe along each end of scarf.

Hat
With MC, cast on 58 sts. Knit 7 rows. Work 1 rep of Stripe pat. With MC, knit 8 rows.
Eyelet row: K1, *yo, k2tog; rep from * to last st, k1.
Knit 7 rows. Bind off all sts. Sew side seam.

Tie
Cut 3 (32-inch) strands of each CC, and 6 of MC. Holding all strands tog, tie an overhand knot approx 2 inches from 1 end. Divide strands into 3 groups, evenly distributing colors. Braid, leaving approx 3½ inches free. Tie overhand knot at end of braid. Trim ends. Weave through eyelets, gather and tie. ■

Un, Deux, Trois

Design by Jil Eaton

Easy as 1, 2, 3, you'll love this funky hat.

Skill Level ◼◼◼◻ INTERMEDIATE

Size
Child (Adult)

Finished Measurement
18 (21) inches

Materials
• Heavy worsted weight yarn: 55 (75) yds orange (A), 15 (25) yds aqua (B), 40 (70) yds powder blue (C)
• Size 9 (5.5mm) straight and double-pointed needles

Earflap
Make 2 as follows:
With 2 dpns and A, cast on 3 sts. Work I-cord as follows: *slide sts to other end of needle and knit 3; rep from * until cord measures 7 (8) inches. Knit 3 rows.
Next row: K1, inc in next st, k1. (4 sts) Knit 3 rows.

Next row: K1, inc in next 2 sts, k1. (6 sts)

Knit 3 rows. Inc 1 st each edge next row, then every 4th row to 14 (18) sts as follows: k1, inc in next st, work to last 2 sts, inc in next st, k1. Bind off.

Hat
With straight needles and A, cast on 72 (84) sts. Knit 3 rows. Work in St st starting with a knit row until piece measures 2 (2½) inches, end WS row. Work 2 rows each B, A, B. Cut A. Work chart until piece measures 6 (8) inches, end WS row.

Bind off sts as follows:
Next row (RS): *Sl 12 (14) sts to dpn. Hold dpn behind primary needle so that wrong sides are facing each other. With another dpn, bind off sts from dpn tog with first 12 (14) sts from needle as follows: Knit first st from dpn tog with first st from needle. **knit next st from dpn tog with next st

from needle, sl first st over 2nd st to bind off; rep from ** until 1 st rem on dpn.

Cut yarn, leaving a long end and pull through rem st. Rep from * twice more. Sew back seam. Pull ends at top of hat to inside and sew center closed. Sew earflaps to edge of hat positioning them 2 (2½) inches in from back seam.

Make 3 (2-inch) pompoms—one each of A, B and C (see page 17). Attach one to each point. ◼

COLOR KEY
⊟ Aqua (B)
☐ Powder blue (C)

CHART A

Blue Skies Hat

Design by Frances Hughes

Kids will love this soft, fluffy hat knitted on big needles.

Skill Level ◼◼◼◻ INTERMEDIATE

Size
Infant's small (large) Instructions are given for smaller size, with larger sizes in parentheses. When only 1 number is given, it applies to all sizes.

Finished Measurements
Circumference: Approx 15 (18) inches

Materials
- Chunky weight polyester novelty yarn (137 yds/50g per ball): 1 ball blue
- Size 10½ (7mm) double-pointed and 16-inch circular needles or size needed to obtain gauge
- Stitch marker

5 BULKY

Gauge
10 sts = 4 inches/10cm in rib pat To save time, take time to check gauge.

Pattern Note
Hat is worked in rnds with 2 strands of yarn held tog.

Hat
With circular needle and 2 strands of yarn, cast on 36 (44) sts. Mark beg of rnd and join without twisting.

Work in rnds of k2, p2 rib until hat measures 5½ (7) inches from beg. On large only, dec 2 sts evenly on last rnd. (36, 42 sts)

Shape top
Rnd 1: *K4, k2tog; rep from * around. (30, 35 sts)

Rnds 2, 4 and 6: Knit.
Rnd 3: *K3, k2tog; rep from * around. (24, 28 sts)
Rnd 5: *K2, k2tog; rep from * around. (18, 21 sts)
Rnd 7: *K1, k2tog; rep from * around. (12, 14 sts)

Cut yarn, leaving an 8-inch end. Thread yarn into tapestry needle and run through rem sts. Pull tight and fasten off securely. ◼

Patriotic Parade

Design by Frances Hughes

Hooray for the Red, White and Blue!

Skill Level ■■■□ INTERMEDIATE

Size
Infant's small (large) Instructions are given for smaller size, with larger size in parentheses. When only 1 number is given, it applies to both sizes.

Finished Measurement
Circumference: 18 (20¼) inches

Materials
- Worsted weight cotton yarn (187 yds/100g per skein): 1 ball each red, blue, white
- Size 7 (4.5mm) 16-inch circular and set of double-pointed needles or size needed to obtain gauge
- Tapestry needle

Gauge
16 sts = 4 inches/10cm in St st
To save time, take time to check gauge.

Hat
With red, cast on 72 (81) sts, and join without twisting.

Knit 8 (10) rnds. [Knit 2 rnds white, 2 rnds red] twice, then knit 1 (3) rnds blue.

Top
Rnds 1–4: Work pat from Chart A.
Rnd 5: With blue, *k2tog, k7; rep from * around. (64, 72 sts)
Rnd 6: With blue, knit.
Rnds 7–10: Work pat from Chart B.
Rnd 11: *K2tog, k6; rep from * around. (56, 63 sts)
Rnd 12 and all even rnds: Knit
Rnd 13: *K2tog, k5; rep from * around. (48, 54 sts)
Rnd 15: *K2tog, k4; rep from * around. (40, 45 sts)
Rnd 17: *K2tog, k3; rep from * around. (32, 36 sts)
Rnd 19: *K2tog, k2; rep from * around. (24, 27 sts)

Rnd 21: *K2tog, k1; rep from * around. (16, 18 sts)

[Rep Rnd 21] once more. (9, 12 sts rem)

Cut yarn leaving an 8-inch tail, thread through sts, draw up and fasten off securely. ∎

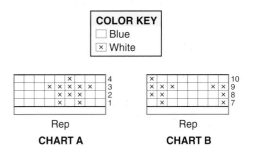

COLOR KEY
☐ Blue
☒ White

Rep
CHART A

Rep
CHART B

Tie-Dye Cap

Design by Laura Polley

Variegated yarn creates a swirl of color for this cap!

Skill Level ◼◼◻◻ EASY

Size
Child's 1–3 (4–7) years
Instructions are given for smaller size, with larger size in parentheses. When only 1 number is given, it applies to both sizes.

Finished Measurements
Head circumference:
20 (22) inches
Length to crown: 4½ (6) inches

Materials
• Worsted weight acrylic yarn (242 yds/4 oz per skein): 1 skein circus variegated
• Size 8 (5mm) straight needle (both sizes)
• 1–3 year size: Size 10 (6mm) double-pointed needles and 16-inch circular needles or size needed to obtain gauge
• 4–7 year size: Size 11 (8mm) double-pointed needles and 16-inch circular needles or size needed to obtain gauge
• Tapestry needle
• Stitch marker

Gauge
1–3 year size: 12 sts = 4 inches/ 10cm in St st with size 10 needles
4–7 year size: 11 sts = 4 inches/10cm in St st with size 11 needles
To save time, take time to check gauge.

Pattern Notes
One 4 oz skein will make a minimum of 2 hats in either size.

A yarn with a color sequence length of approx 60 inches will give best color swirl effect.

Cap
With appropriate circular needle for desired size, cast on 60 sts. Place marker and join without twisting.

Work in rnds of St st (knit every rnd) until hat measures approx 4½ (6) inches from beg.

Shape Top
Note: Switch to dpns as needed.
Rnd 1: *K8, k2tog; rep from * around. (54 sts)
Rnd 2: *K7, k2tog; rep from * around. (48 sts)
Rnd 3: *K6, k2tog; rep from * around (42 sts)
Rnd 4: *K5, k2tog; rep from * around. (36 sts)
Rnd 5: *K4, k2tog; rep from * around. (30 sts)
Rnd 6: *K3, k2tog; rep from * around. (24 sts)
Rnd 7: *K2, k2tog; rep from * around. (18 sts)
Rnd 8: *K1, k2tog; rep from * around. (12 sts)
Rnd 9: *K2tog; rep from * around. (6 sts)

Cut yarn, leaving a 5-inch tail. With tapestry needle, weave tail through rem sts and draw up tightly to close top.

Finishing
Hold hat so cast-on edge is at top. With size 8 needle, RS facing, loosely pick up and knit 2 sts from first rnd worked after cast on. *With left forefinger or extra size 8 needle, pass first picked up st over 2nd picked up st. Loosely pick up and knit 1 st to left of st on needle. Rep from * until 1 lp rem on needle. Cut yarn and draw through lp. ∎

Yarn Information

Each project in this leaflet was made using various weights of yarn. Any brand of specified weight of yarn may be used. It is best to refer to the yardage/meters when determining how many balls or skeins to purchase. Remember, to arrive at the finished size, it is the GAUGE/TENSION that is important, not the brand of yarn. For your convenience, listed below are the specific yarns used to create our photography models.

Page 4: Stunning Scarves—Sample projects were completed with Melody (100 percent acrylic) color #09732 hot pink (short scarf) #09714 mango or #09742 peacock (long scarves) and Cha Cha (100 percent nylon) color #02003 bebop (short scarf) #02004 salsa or 02002 Vegas (long scarves) from Patons Yarns

Page 6: Greek Eyelash Scarf—Sample project was completed with Stylecraft Eskimo DK (100 percent polyester eyelash yarn) color #5480 kingfisher from S.R. Kertzer

Page 7: Plush Scarf—Sample project was completed with Wool-Ease Thick & Quick (80 percent acrylic/20 percent wool) color #187 goldenrod and Chenille Thick & Quick (91 percent acrylic/9 percent rayon) color #230 jade print from Lion Brand Yarn Co.

Page 8: Comfy Ruby Scarf—Sample project was completed with Jewel Box (64 percent acrylic/20 percent rayon/16 percent polyester) color #0020 ruby from Caron International

Page 9: Warm Ribbed Scarf— Sample project was completed with Silk Garden (45 percent silk/45 percent kid mohair/10 percent lamb's wool) color #82 from Noro Yarns

Page 10: Holiday Warmer— Sample project was completed with Patons Décor (75 percent acrylic/25 percent wool) color #1714 barn red (MC), #1672 gray heather (A), #1614 white (B) and #1637 rich sage green (C) from Spinrite Yarn

Page 12: Zigzag Scarves—Adult sample project was completed with Melody (solid: 84 percent acrylic/16 percent nylon) color #09742 (MC), (variegated: 68 percent acrylic/32 percent nylon) color #09713 happy days (CC) from Patons Yarns. Child sample project was completed with Astra (100 percent acrylic) color #8714 mango (MC) and #88761 Kool Aid (CC) from Patons Yarns

Page 14: Cozy Amethyst Scarf— Sample project was completed with Jewel Box (64 percent acrylic/20 percent rayon/16 percent polyester) color #0015 amethyst from Caron International

Page 15: Autumn Lace Scarf— Sample project was completed with Artful Yarns Portrait (70 percent mohair/25 percent viscose/5 percent polyester) color #104 from JCA Inc. and Katia Gatsby (77 percent viscose/15 percent polyamide/8 percent polyester) color #13 brown from KFI

Page 16: Fringed Scarf—Sample project was completed with Imagine (80 percent acrylic/20 percent mohair) color #171 moss from Lion Brand Yarn Co.

Page 19: Evening Intrigue Scarf— Sample project was completed with Dune (30 percent acrylic/11 percent nylon/41 percent mohair/6 percent metal/12 percent rayon) color #82 and Aura (100 percent nylon) color #707502 from Trendsetter Yarns.

Page 20: Diamond Twist Scarf— Sample project was completed with Red Heart TLC (100 percent acrylic) color #5915 claret from Coats & Clark.

Page 23: Cotillion Scarf—Sample project was completed with Glitterspun (60 percent acrylic/27 percent Cupro/13 percent polyester) color #113 ruby (A) and Fun Fur (100 percent polyester) color #113 red (B) from Lion Brand Yarn Co.

Page 24: Shimmering Scarf— Sample project was completed with Aura (100 percent nylon) color #8281 mulberry from Trendsetter Yarns.

Page 26: Glitzy Scarf—Sample project was completed with Adriafil Stars (50 percent viscose/50 percent nylon) color #40 from Plymouth Yarn Co.

Page 27: Sparkle Scarf—Sample project was completed with Metallica (85 percent rayon/15 percent metallic) color #1002 silver from Berroco.

Page 29: Faux Fur Collar & Cuffs—Sample project was completed with Fun Fur (100 percent polyester) colors #153 black, #134 copper and #126 chocolate from Lion Brand Yarn Co.

Page 30: Chic Cowl & Cuffs—Sample project was completed with Eye Lash (100 percent nylon) color #35315 flash from Bernat Yarns.

Page 31: Ready for Winter—Sample project was completed with Hand-dyed Wool Top (100 percent wool) from Lorna's Laces.

Page 32: Ski Band Stripes— Sample project was completed with X-press (60 percent merino wool/40 percent acrylic) color #3611 green (A) from Berroco Inc. and Baby (100 percent merino wool) color #1 white (B) from Tahki/Stacy Charles Inc.

Page 34: School Colors Scarf & Hat—Sample project was completed with Encore (75 percent acrylic/25 percent wool) #133 blue (MC), #146 off-white (CC) from Plymouth Yarn Co.

Page 36: Big Needle Winter Set— Sample project was completed with Bella (50 percent merino wool/50 percent acrylic) color #1725 celestial from Patons Yarns.

Page 38: A Touch of Color Hat & Scarf—Sample project was completed with Lamb's Pride Bulky (85 percent wool/15 percent mohair) color # M06 deep charcoal (A) from Brown Sheep Co. and Alpaca Boucle color #112 (B) from Plymouth Yarn Co.

Page 40: Quick & Easy Roll-Brim Hat—Sample project was completed with Kureyon (100 percent wool) color #40 from Noro Yarns.

Page 43: Funky Hemmed Hat— Sample project was completed with Lamb's Pride Superwash Bulky (100 percent wool) color #SW05 (A) from Brown Sheep Co. and Filatura di Crosa Adhoe (50 percent wool/30 percent polyester/20 percent acrylic) color #2 (B) from Tahki/Stacy Charles Inc.

Page 44: Quick Cozy Hat—Sample project was completed with Paparazzi (25 percent wool/75 percent acrylic) color #5259 variegated (A) from Tahki/Stacy Charles Inc. and Lamb's Pride Superwash Bulky (100 percent wool) color #SW63 midnight pine (B) from Brown Sheep Co.

Page 46: Warm & Toasty Stocking Cap—Sample project was completed with Nature Spun Sport (100 percent wool) color #701 stone (MC), #730 natural (A) and #N20 Arctic moss (B) from Brown Sheep Co.

Page 48: Casual Cables Ski Tam—Sample project was completed in Jiffy (100 percent acrylic) color #099 fisherman from Lion Brand Yarn Co.

Page 51: Striped Tiptop Hats—Sample project was completed with Lamb's Pride Bulky (85 percent wool/15 percent mohair) from Brown Sheep Co.

Page 52: Candles Triangular Scarf—Sample project was completed with Katia Idea Mix Knitting Ribbon (45 percent cotton/45 percent rayon/10 percent linen) color light blue.

Page 55: Grape Confetti Hat & Scarf Set—Sample project was completed with Rimini Rainbow (40 percent wool/60 percent acrylic) color #05 purple rainbow from Plymouth Yarn Co.

Page 56: Stripy Mohair Scarf & Hat—Sample project was completed with Mohair Classic (78 percent mohair/13 percent wool/9 percent nylon) color #1488 pink (MC), #1487 orange (A), #1110 purple (B), #8222 yellow (C), #1486 blue (D) #1485 lime (E) from Berroco.

Page 58: Un, Deux, Trois—Sample project was completed with Manos del Uruguay, color #69 hibiscus (A), #05 aqua (B), powder blue (C).

Page 60: Blue Skies Hat—Sample project was completed with Sirdar Snowflake Chunky Magic (100 percent polyester) color #415 blue from Knitting Fever.

Page 61: Patriotic Parade—Sample project was completed with Reynolds Saucy (100 percent cotton) from JCA/Reynolds, Inc.

Page 62: Tie-Dye Cap—Sample project was completed with Red Heart Kids (100 percent acrylic) color #2945 bikini variegated from Coats & Clark.

Standard Abbreviations

[ ] work instructions within brackets as many times as directed

( ) work instructions within parentheses in the place directed

** repeat instructions following the asterisks as directed

* repeat instructions following the single asterisk as directed

" inch(es)

approx approximately

beg begin/beginning

CC contrasting color

ch chain stitch

cm centimeter(s)

cn cable needle

dec decrease/decreases/ decreasing

dpn(s) double-pointed needle(s)

g gram

inc increase/increases/ increasing

k knit

k2tog knit 2 stitches together

LH left hand

lp(s) loop(s)

m meter(s)

M1 make one stitch

MC main color

mm millimeter(s)

oz ounce(s)

p purl

pat(s) pattern(s)

p2tog purl 2 stitches together

psso pass slipped stitch over

rem remain/remaining

rep repeat(s)

rev St st reverse stockinette stitch

RH right hand

rnd(s) rounds

RS right side

skp slip, knit, pass stitch over—one stitch decreased

sk2p slip 1, knit 2 together, pass slip stitch over the knit 2 together; 2 stitches have been decreased

sl slip

sl 1k slip 1 knitwise

sl 1p slip 1 purlwise

sl st slip stitch(es)

ssk slip, slip, knit these 2 stitches together—a decrease

st(s) stitch(es)

St st stockinette stitch/ stocking stitch

tbl through back loop(s)

tog together

WS wrong side

wyib with yarn in back

wyif with yarn in front

yd(s) yard(s)

yfwd yarn forward

yo yarn over

Skill Levels

■□□□□ **BEGINNER**

Projects for first-time knitters using basic knit and purl stitches. Minimal shaping.

■■□□□ **EASY**

Projects using basic stitches, repetitive stitch patterns, simple color changes and simple shaping and finishing.

■■■□□ **INTERMEDIATE**

Projects with a variety of stitches, such as basic cables and lace, simple intarsia, double-pointed needles and knitting in the round needle techniques, mid-level shaping and finishing.

■■■■□ **EXPERIENCED**

Projects using advanced techniques and stitches, such as short rows, Fair Isle, more intricate intarsia, cables, lace patterns and numerous color changes.

Big Book of Knit Hats & Scarves for Everyone

© 2005, 2004, 2003, 2002, 2001 House of White Birches, 306 East Parr Road, Berne, IN 46711, (260) 589-4000. Customer_Service@whitebirches.com. Made in USA.

We have made every effort to ensure that the instructions in this book are complete and accurate. We cannot be responsible for human error, typographical mistakes or variations in individual work. The designs in this book are protected by copyright; however, you may make the designs for your personal use. This right is surpassed when the designs are made by employees or sold commercially.

ISBN: 1-57486-584-6

Published by Leisure Arts, Inc., 5701 Ranch Drive, Little Rock, Arkansas 72223.

1 2 3 4 5 6 7 8 9

Standard Yarn Weight System

Categories of yarn, gauge ranges, and recommended needle sizes

Yarn Weight Symbol & Category Names	1 SUPER FINE	2 FINE	3 LIGHT	4 MEDIUM	5 BULKY	6 SUPER BULKY
Type of Yarns in Category	Sock, Fingering, Baby	Sport, Baby	DK, Light Worsted	Worsted, Afghan, Aran	Chunky, Craft, Rug	Bulky, Roving
Knit Gauge* Ranges in Stockinette Stitch to 4 inches	21–32 sts	23–26 sts	21–24 sts	16–20 sts	12–15 sts	6–11 sts
Recommended Needle in Metric Size Range	2.25–3.25mm	3.25–3.75mm	3.75–4.5mm	4.5–5.5mm	5.5–8mm	8mm
Recommended Needle U.S. Size Range	1 to 3	3 to 5	5 to 7	7 to 9	9 to 11	11 and larger

* GUIDELINES ONLY: The above reflect the most commonly used gauges and needle sizes for specific yarn categories.